Leicester

A Second Selection

IN OLD PHOTOGRAPHS

'Grin & Bare It' was just one of many saucy shows staged at the Palace Theatre. The Austin A35 vans and the Ford Prefect that can be seen parked in front of the theatre bring back memories of a more carefree era of motoring.

Leicester

A Second Selection

IN OLD PHOTOGRAPHS

DAVID R. BURTON

Alan Sutton Publishing Limited
Phoenix Mill · Far Thrupp · Stroud
Gloucestershire

First Published 1994

British Library Cataloguing in Publication Data.
A catalogue record for this book is available from
the British Library.

ISBN 0-7509-0683-9

Typeset in 9/10 Sabon.
Typesetting and origination by
Alan Sutton Publishing Limited.
Printed in Great Britain by
Redwood Books, Trowbridge.

This view taken in about 1902 shows the
ruins of Huntingdon Tower – the
erstwhile town house of the Earl of
Huntingdon – about to be demolished to
allow road widening in the High Street.
Whitcher Menswear now stands close to
where the tower once stood.

Contents

Gallowtree Gate, *c.* 1950. For many, this is an image of the city as they prefer to remember it; somehow, the ambience then was more agreeable than it is today. Finlay's tobacconist can be seen on the left, F.W. Woolworth's on the right.

Introduction

In September 1993 my first ever book, *Leicester in Old Photographs*, was published by Alan Sutton Publishing using material drawn mainly from my own collection of old postcards. By Christmas the book had sold out. This success caused the publisher to ask me to compile a second selection. This differs from the first by drawing much of its material from the photographic archives of the *Leicester Mercury*.

The process of selecting and compiling these images has brought back many memories for me, both of people and places: the area where I once lived, Wyngate Drive, Hinckley Road, the waste land next to the Co-op in Mostyn Street; the shops on Hinckley Road (Heards, Rawsons and Silvers); the Hunters speedway team, the Leicester Query Motorcycle Club and Jack Shaw with his Vincent; going to Morley Clark the tailor in Loseby Lane with alterations from Whitcher's (known as the Magnet), where I worked; the Beehive shop and the strange overhead cash system; working in C Department at R. Rowley & Co. of Queen Street with Ken Mascord and Joyce Keevill, Flo Sewell and Roy Treddell, my girlfriend at the time Nora Russell, and 'fo me' Clarke in the despatch department. The nights at the Palace Theatre variety shows – 1s 6d in the 'Gods' (I earned £3 a week in 1950).

I hope the pictures on the pages that follow will revive your memories as much as they have mine. I hope, too, they are happy ones and that you enjoy my book.

If any old friends wish to get in touch with me, I can be contacted through the publisher.

A stream of trams and buses make their way along Granby Street. Bishop Street is on the right.

We often think of traffic jams as a phenomenon of the late twentieth century, but this scene of traffic chaos in the lower High Street in the 1900s proves otherwise. Lloyds Bank is on the right.

SECTION ONE

Shops and Businesses

The High Street in 1956. It was at about this time that I worked for Whitcher's Menswear (known as the Magnet) seen here on the left of the picture. Every boy going to secondary school who purchased a school uniform here was given a small magnet in a box. The uniform department was run by Miss Hardy. The ground floor was for shirts and outfitting, with suits downstairs in the basement. The first floor served as the warehouse for eleven shops and the second floor was all offices. During my time with the company I worked with many people including Tony Whitcher, Gordon Grouse, Peter Shoreland and Javen Smith, Pop Newman, Eric Stokes, John (Werner Muhlenfield), Miss D. Dunham and Michael Whitcher.

Arthur Whitcher aged seventy-five and his wife Marcelle with their son Walter Whitcher (left foreground) on the occasion of the wedding of Tony Whitcher. Arthur Whitcher came to Leicester in 1901 from a family business in Newport and Cowes on the Isle of Wight. When his Swiss wife Marcelle and sons Walter and Stanley joined him shortly afterwards they all lived above the shop. Stanley Whitcher was very involved with the Leicester Thursday Rugby Club.

No. 45 High Street, *c.* 1901. Arthur Whitcher cycled to Leicester from Newport, Isle of Wight, and set up the men's outfitters which today can be found at Nos 49/51 High Street. Michael J. Whitcher, Arthur Whitcher's grandson, runs the business today with great-grandson Mark Whitcher as a director. Tony Whitcher, Mark's father, remains a director although he is retired.

George Needham takes down the shutters of his clock, watch and jewellery shop at 77 Southgate Street. E.L. Woods kept the newsagent's shop just along the road, where many customers called for sweets and newspapers before catching the bus at the old Midland Red depot.

Southgate Street/The Newarkes corner fell to the hammers of the demolition men in the 1930s.

The Silver Arcade in 1908 with Kellett's shop along the front. The 6½d bazaar was obviously a popular place to shop because they boasted that nothing cost over 6½d.

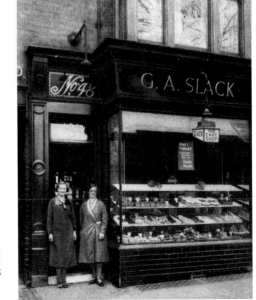

No. 48 Hinckley Road as it was in 1933, 'The Cake Shop'. The lady on the left is Barbara Harris (née Gadsby) and on the right can be seen Ethel Langford. A large loaf cost 4½d and hot cross buns were seven for 6d; 4½d would buy a quarter-pound of Linnell's potted meat.

Foxons, the newsagent and stationer, at 39 Churchgate. The shop traded for more than 100 years and R. Farquett was the last owner.

John and Thomas Spencer started their business in the Market Place in 1853. The passageway on the right leads to the White Lion Hotel where Elizabeth Wherry was the licensee in its last years. Mr Winn next door, a keen amateur photographer, is said to have taken this picture in 1900.

This is the hardware shop of W.T. Mills in East Park Road, pictured in about 1935. Here you could buy a tin bath for 5s 6d, galvanized dustbins for 7s 6d, buckets for 1s and vinegar at 2d a pint. The average weekly wage at this time was £2 13s 3d.

A shop to beat all shops – the pawnbroker. This one was at 182 Humberstone Road. A familiar sight in many towns and cities, pawnbroking thrived at the turn of the century.

The Beehive shop in Silver Street sold haberdashery, ladies' wear, sheets and blankets.

What memories are evoked by this picture of the interior of the Beehive shop. I always wondered how those large wooden balls stayed on the track whizzing down the shop. And how exactly did they find their way back to the right counter? Here we see Miss H.L. Grimsley behind the counter operating the cash machine.

Worthington's Ltd, at the corner of Beatrice Road and Oban Street, was a grocer's. The shopfront is pictured here in the 1920s, with the staff posing in the doorway for the camera.

Pre-war in Hotel Street. Just look at those prices – a packet of five Woodbines for 2d, port and sherry at 3s 9d a bottle. A secondhand 1931 Morris Cowley saloon car could be bought for £22 10s, while 10s would fill it with petrol.

The Frog Island post office, *c.* 1904. Mr Aldwinckle, the postmaster, stands in the doorway.

A group of children standing outside the Biddulph Street dairy in the early 1900s. The boy wearing the boater to the right of the shop doorway is Walter Willett who, at the age of eighteen, gave his life for his country in the First World War.

Joseph Foster ran this shop at 22 Belgrave Gate in the late nineteenth century, with branches in Nottingham and Loughborough. George Foster, his son, was later to become his errand boy. Joseph lived with his wife at 94 Evington Drive.

Another view of Worthington's cash stores in Beatrice Road, this time in 1930. The manager C.H. Ward can be seen on the left. Eggs were five for a shilling, with bacon at 1s 3d a pound.

The long established Leicester firm of Billson & Grant (originally R. Billson) was founded in the 1830s. They made rope and canvas sheets for lorries which they sold from their premises on the corner of Belgrave Gate and Charles Street. In 1982 the company moved to premises at Anstey.

J. Biddles in Humberstone Road, 'the old original tripe shop', was established in 1832 as one of the many tripe dealers in the city and was still going strong when this photograph was taken in 1967. A tripe dresser, Sidney Baxter, started in the business at the age of nine.

No. 72B Hinckley Road photographed before the Second World War. Elijah Warwick (on the right) built his own cycles and repaired punctures despite having lost his sight in a gas attack in the First World War. The 'Warwick' cycle was named after him and became much sought after. Mr Warwick's nephew, Roland Hill, worked as a driver with the *Leicester Mercury* until his retirement.

Applegate Street with St Nicholas's church on the right. J. Friswell cycles was run by
Mrs Pether (Mr Friswell's daughter) and her husband in more recent years. They lived
on Wyngate Drive and their son John went to school with me.

Belvoir Street in the late 1940s. On the left can be seen Viv Crosby's café, on the right Robotham's, Hill & Hemming Menswear, and Cowling's on the corner with a billiard hall above the shop. The author worked at Hill & Hemming in 1951 aged sixteen.

The shop interior of Hill & Hemming Menswear in Belvoir Street where I worked with Gordon Jones, and my bosses Jack Hill and Ray Hemming.

The late Jack Hill of Hill & Hemming in Belvoir Street. He lived in Holmfield Avenue, Stoneygate, and came originally from Melton Mowbray, as did my father.

Gordon Jones and Jack Hill of Hill & Hemming, leaning on a new Hillman Minx which boasted a column gear change (although not a very positive one as I remember).

Welford Road, *c.* 1916. The queue is outside a butcher's shop at No. 58, A. Upton & Son, where the proprietor was one F.W. Squires. Next door was the fishmonger Skeet & Son, and then the bootmaker Jessie W. Le Butt.

This picture shows Mr and Mrs White outside their shop in Upper Conduit Street during the 1920s. It stood opposite Hillcrest, the old workhouse, and Mr White ran the ironmonger's while his wife had a china shop next door. At the time of writing (1994) Mr White's son, C.W. White, was eighty-four and living in Northampton.

Withers, the Loseby Lane antique dealers, was established in 1860. When this picture was taken in 1962 the company was about to move to new premises on the London Road.

Leicester cattle market in about 1975, during a lamb sale. Jim Reynolds, wearing the flat cap, was appeals chairman of the Royal Agricultural Benevolent Institution at the time this picture was taken.

The city's old fish market was designed by the respected local architect William Millcan.

John Collins was one of the oldest fishmongers and poulterers in the market. The business had been established on a wooden stall in 1864 and handed down through the family.

This watercolour of the Leicester market is by A.H. Findlay and is described as 'An interesting early view of Leicester market, *c.* 1930'.

A pre-1915 scene in Halford Street wholesale fruit and vegetable market where the day started at 4 a.m., wet or fine, with lorries and carts coming in from the surrounding countryside. A. Marks was one of the leading wholesalers of the day.

Early morning in Halford Street wholesale fruit and vegetable market. A familiar name is on the van – Ratcliffe's, while that of A. Marks is on the hand cart.

Robert Ford and John Russell hold the 'time-bottle' found walled-up since 1888 in the original children's hospital. The bottle was discovered while digging foundations for the Royal Infirmary extension in 1954. It contained a programme of the laying of the foundation stone, a copy of the *Leicester Daily Post* and other historic documents. An advertisement carried on the front of the newspaper was for R. Morley & Sons of Cheapside.

The *Leicester Mercury* 'time-bottle' was placed in the Royal Infirmary Foundation Stone in 1954.

St Martin's seen here in 1974. No. 3 St Martin's was the first home of the *Leicester Mercury* in 1874.

This is the back of the *Leicester Mercury* offices at 3 St Martin's, also in 1974, where the newspaper was produced, printed and distributed.

The Albion Street offices of the *Leicester Mercury* decorated for the coronation of Queen Elizabeth II on 2 June 1953. The *Mercury*'s offices were here from 1890 to 1966.

The *Mercury*'s fleet of vans, registration numbers JF9951 onwards, displayed on the ground where the present offices stand.

The headquarters of Wolsey Ltd in King Street. The late Leslie Miller, chairman of Wolsey Ltd until 1967, was instrumental in converting properties to form the New Walk Centre.

Cardinal Wolsey's statue is flanked by long service employees, each of whom had worked fifty years at Abbey Meadow Mills Factory, at the presentation ceremony in 1972. Left to right: Hugh Kendrick, Harold Rayfield, D.R. Graham (director), Harold Waterfield, A.G. Scrimshaw (managing director), Fred Bayliss, Jack Olpin, Frank Tattersall.

C. Shipley was in charge of the despatch department at Kendall & Sons which had some 50,000 umbrellas in stock. Some of the handles were made at the company's own handle factory in London, while others were imported from Italy and France.

Thomas Kirby (centre), his family and staff at about the turn of the century, outside the Highfields dairy. The business was later known as Kirby & West and operated from West Bridge.

Some of the staff of J. Jelley Builders pictured outside the company's first premises at 43 Shenton Street. It was formed in 1889 by James Jelley who was born in 1865; his son Herbert joined the company in 1919 after war service in the Leicestershire Yeomanry.

Some of the employees of J. Jelley who have helped to build the reputation of the company.

Herbert Jelley, son of the founder, who was responsible for expanding the business into the house-building market.

Florence Jelley, later Mrs F. Stubbings, ran the office and sales side of the business.

A typical Jelley-built house, 103 Wyngate Drive, where I lived as a boy. Before its development for housing, this area was covered by allotments. We had a well in our back garden and during the war years an Anderson shelter which we shared with the Thornley family next door.

The deposit of £10 for 103 Wyngate Drive, dated 4 May 1934. The house cost £650. I was told 'Jelley built, well built'.

A close-up view of the 'time-bottle' containing an advertisement for R. Morley & Sons, for whom both my mother and father worked.

A busy scene at an industrial premises in the 1920s: this is Raven's hosiery factory in Wharf Street.

The front entrance of R. Rowley & Co.'s premises. Through the archway was a cobbled yard. The company had its own print shop and machine repair workshop: material went in, was made up, pressed, boxed, labelled and sent out. It is now part of Courtauld's.

R. Rowley & Co. Ltd: Mr B. Norton is here seen operating an RTR machine in the Queen Street factory.

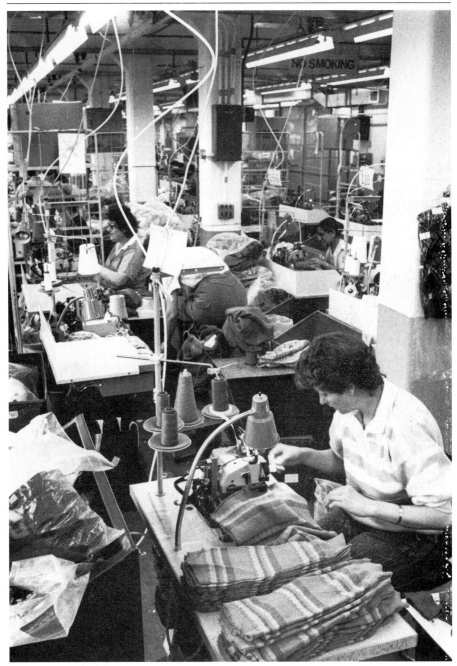

The Rowley Group's factory in Queen Street. Established in 1867, it remained a family business until the 1960s when Courtauld's took it over. I worked here in C Department in 1951 with Ken Mascord, Roy Treddell, Joyce Keevill, Flo Sewell and Nora Russell.

Robert Rowley, the founder and chairman from 1867 to 1936 of the Rowley empire which had five factories employing 1,400 people. Rowley was the son of a woodworker from Wisbech, Cambridgeshire.

T.S. Rowley, the son of Robert Rowley, was chairman from 1936 to 1937.

L. Craufurd Robertson, a grandson of Robert Rowley, succeeded T.S. Rowley as chairman in 1937.

A stocking knitter's cottage like those in Great Glen and Thurmaston. These workers made up the goods which Robert Rowley took to his first factory in Wigston Street to sell.

A typical knitter's frame which could be used at home by outworkers.

Belvoir Street. Robotham's served the needs of Leicester mums for sixty-six years. During the war the top floor of this row of shops was opened up inside, making it easily accessible from end to end in the event of fire caused by incendiary bombs. Stirrup pumps were also kept up there as a precaution.

SECTION TWO
Streets of Leicester

The double tram tracks visible in this view made it difficult for motor vehicles to overtake trams. This picture was taken before 1930 in Belgrave Gate just below the Charles Street junction.

High Street and Highcross Street, showing the Family Fry Pan. It was still there in the 1940s.

Butler's chemist shop at the corner of Carts Lane and the High Street in about 1910. I remember it later as a cycle shop when I worked in the High Street.

Loseby Lane in 1958 was a small but busy street. Here the month is November and the Christmas decorations are already up on the Co-op. Lee's wool shop is on the right of the picture; the sandwiches from the café next door were excellent.

An unusual traffic problem in Loseby Lane in 1954, caused by a tank on a low-loader.

Another view of Belvoir Street opposite the 'pork pie' chapel. On the right can be seen Joseph Johnson's shop where I spent a short time working in the menswear department. Crawford Johnson was the managing director, John Caws was the manager; Mr Valentine and Mr Pennington worked in the clothing department, with Mr Akers and Mr Clee on the ground floor.

A busy scene looking up towards the High Street in 1939.

Trams and a pony and trap mixing safely side by side on Granby Street in about 1917.

The shop on the corner of Granby Street in this view of about 1906 is Turner & Jaques. Jack Hill of Hill & Hemming worked there at one time.

Granby Street, *c.* 1904. The Imperial Typewriter Co. is evident in the foreground, with the Spencer corset shop next door.

The postmark on this card of Granby Street is 1952, but I think the picture itself dates from much earlier. The Wellington Hotel on the corner was often used by local businessmen at lunchtimes.

The temporary war memorial in the Municipal Square in about 1935. Judging from this photograph high-seated cycles and cloth caps were the order of the day.

This unusual postcard view of the Municipal buildings was posted in South Wigston in 1951.

The Leicester market by the Corn Exchange steps, *c.* 1906. Posted from Barry Dock in South Wales, the correspondents on the back of this card say they have 'not heard of the Splott [near Cardiff] folks since Christmas'.

Leicester Market Place photographed from an unusual angle. The Leicester Meat Co. on the corner can be clearly seen, but this area is now very much changed.

The market square was full to capacity to hear the proclamation of King George V on 10 May 1910.

Leicester fair was held in Humberstone Gate in this photograph dating from the 1920s. I see the law went about in pairs even then.

Taken in the late 1890s, this picture shows the cheese fair held twice a year on the south side of the Corn Exchange. Bedded safely in straw on farm carts, the cheeses – Leicester and Stilton – were brought in to the city by the farmers who then stayed overnight at the White Swan, Bull's Head and Saracen's Head. Swain's of Highcross Street was one of the oldest cheese dealers in the city.

The cobbled High Street just below Union Street and Ye Olde Crown Inn, whose licensee was Stephen Cooper. The road was cobbled then and there were gas lamps on the shops.

Leicester viewed from the air, 1972. The Town Hall Square and the market are easy to discern.

The Dover Café in Dover Street was often frequented by staff of the *Leicester Mercury* from their old offices in Albion Street. Although it was known as the 'reporters' den', 'The Dover' was also used by many staff from the nearby weights and measures department.

Humberstone Gate in about 1960, showing The Old Stag and Pheasant, The Tower and the Yorkshire Penny Bank. This part of Humberstone Gate was later pulled down to make way for the Haymarket Centre.

A good picture often needs no caption. Look at the detail in this photograph of Frog Island for example, taken before 1904: the Frears' delivery van, the shop signs and the people.

This decorative arch was erected across the Haymarket to commemorate the visit of the Prince and Princess of Wales (Edward VII and Queen Alexandra) when they came to open the Abbey Park on 29 May 1882. The one-horse tram is on its way to Belgrave.

Welford Road in about 1928, a quiet road by today's standards.

An open-topped horse-drawn bus makes its way along the London Road in about 1903.

This view of the London Road in the early 1900s makes a sharp contrast with that of today. In those days it was a very popular residential area, but shops now occupy the ground floors.

This view of Upper Conduit Street in about 1948 includes three properties which Leicester Highways Committee purchased as part of a street improvement scheme. In the background is the narrow junction with Sparkenhoe Street.

Looking up London Road from outside the Midland station in 1963 after the road-widening scheme.

Shell BP House on the corner of London Road and Station Street, *c.* 1951. The building also once housed the Old Wyvern Hotel.

The lower section of London Road in 1956. Victoria Road church can be seen in the distance, with Prebend Street on the left and one of the old alterable 'No Waiting' signs.

London Road in the 1950s before it was widened.

Applegate Street in 1955, looking down towards the Castle Gardens.

Applegate Street, this time in about 1880. The opening on the right was the turning to West Bridge; ahead led to Redcross Street. The house and shop straight ahead was L.P. North meat stores at 2 West Bridge Street. Around the corner there was a corn merchant, next door to which could be found the famous bakehouse of Elizabeth Perkins.

A quiet urban scene in Applegate Street during the 1950s. What a contrast it makes to the same scene today. Friswell's cycle shop can be seen on the left.

Charles Street, pictured here in the early 1930s, is the site of the municipal offices today.

Charles Street before road widening took place. Thomas Firth's building is the tall structure on the left.

Charles Street at its junction with the corner of Halford Street, *c.* 1910.

A part of Woodgate including the old Robin Hood Inn at around the turn of the century. A directory of 1815 lists two inns in Woodgate, The Abbey and The Golden Fleece, but not a Robin Hood as in the picture. The houses shown here pre-date the year 1815.

Customers pose for the camera outside The Dolphin Inn, on the corner of Lichfield Street and Burleys Lane, where William Payne was the landlord.

This picture is believed to be of Humberstone Road where the lady with the shawl and cap is walking past Harry Drake's store. The sign above the shop reads 'Quality is the test of cheapness'. Note the perambulator.

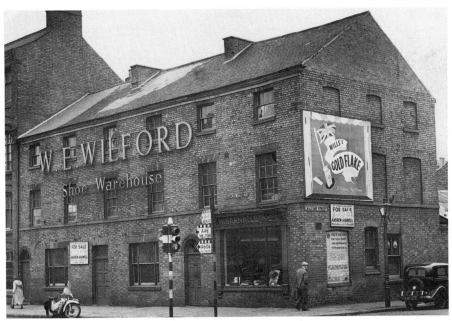

Wilford's Shoe Warehouse in Charles Street on the corner of Halford Street. Parked beside the kerb on the left is a Velocette LE motorcycle; the shop in the centre of the picture is H. Barnacle, which sold typewriters.

The old Town Hall library and West Front at St Martin's.

The Granby Hall where skating, exhibitions and fairs all took place and have done so for years. This is the queue for the thirty-third Home Life Exhibition.

Melton Road at the Loughborough turn, *c.* 1935. This road has changed less than some others in the city and remains fairly easily recognizable today. The same cannot be said for the cars, however. They are, from left to right: a Standard saloon, a Bullnose Morris, a check-grilled Vauxhall and an Austin Ten.

A street scene in one of the poorer areas of Leicester during the 1920s. With the economic depression that followed the First World War life must have been hard, but even so there are a lot of smiles evident in this picture.

The points of interest in this view of Queen's Road in about 1960 are the National Provincial Bank and the cars – no fewer than five Morris Minors can be counted.

At the corner of Causeway Lane and White Street, a group of regulars stand outside the Charles Napier public house in about 1913, where they sold Hole's Newark ales.

This is Walter Newbury outside his mother's shop and dairy in the Highfields. The shop next door sold maids' uniforms, lace collars and cuffs.

This interesting picture of the Haymarket was taken in about 1880, but just what the occasion was I do not know.

This photograph of the Haymarket dates from 1937 although it looks much older. The main building in the picture is John Burton & Sons, photographers.

This card was sent from 12 Bismark Street to Mrs Flo Cooling in Skegness in 1908. The children in the picture are from No. 12. It is believed that the street's name was changed to Beaconsfield Road in about 1916.

The West End

An etching of the city in 1840 as seen from Knighton Hill.

Western Road, looking towards Braunstone Gate in the 1960s. The grocer's shop on the left of the picture is on the corner of Gaul Street and opposite is the Equity shoe factory, Potter's the ironmongers and the adult school. When Mr and Mrs Albert Sharman lived in this street (the fourth house on the left), the rent was 14s a week.

The junction of Narborough Road and Hinckley Road. Beyond the railings can be seen Latimer's furnishers; the gents' lavatory is underground below the railings.

The junction of Hinckley Road and Narborough Road, looking towards Braunstone Gate and Western Boulevard, known also as the Five Lights.

The Narborough Road junction on a wet and windy day in 1951. It is evident from this picture that the road had been only recently altered as the pedestrian crossing goes only as far as the police box and lavatory.

I believe this view of the Narborough Road in about 1930 was taken from a point just past the Upperton Road crossroads.

Narborough Road junction and the horse trough. In 1903 George and Annis Bills from Australia paid for a number of horse troughs in Britain and Australia, of which this was one.

Narborough Road, *c.* 1914. Today very little has changed although the trams and their lines have gone, and the trees have matured. The chapel on the right and the open-topped tram are a sign of the times.

Narborough Road in 1961. The interest lies here with the car in the foreground, an Austin Cambridge Farina. I still have a rear light in my garage, the only bit left of mine.

West Bridge from the railway bridge which crosses the canal at Bath Lane. There has been a bridge on this site since 1325, although this one was built in 1890 at a cost of about £4,000.

King Richard's Road in 1965, looking up the hill from the corner of Tudor Road.

Stretton Road, *c.* 1906. Yet another postcard from Edie to Mrs Cooling who lived at No. 70.

Tudor Road at the junction with King Richard's Road seen here in 1958. I often passed this way when I went to the Tudor cinema, which I seem to remember was further down the road on the left.

Another view looking up Hinckley Road showing Mason's shoe shop. The Westminster Bank can be seen on the right; the Trustee Savings Bank was on the left.

The junction of Hinckley Road and Fosse Road, c. 1905.

Hinckley Road in 1963 as seen from the junction with Narborough Road. I once owned an Austin A35 van like the one on the left of the picture. A little further up the road on the left was Tompkins' tobacconist. Mr Tompkins' daughter Jo is my sister-in-law.

Hinckley Road in 1962 near the junction with Narborough Road.

A tree-lined Narborough Road in 1960; it was one of the best shopping areas in the West End at this time.

Hinckley Road in 1961. I can remember Forryan's the chemist but very few other shops.

This is one of the few photographs of the Hinckley Road shopping area between Kirby Road and Mostyn Street. On the left was Dr Stewart Mann's house and surgery, then a few shops, then Dunster Street with its chip shop, and opposite Oldham's the newsagents. Worthington's was on the corner, then the Western Park garage. On the right was John Silver the chemist, the post office, and Boot's the chemist. Further down the road could be found Rawson's greengrocers, Heard's butchers, Skerritt's ironmongers, Ingham's fishmongers and many more besides.

The junction of Hinckley Road, Wyngate Drive (to the left) and Woodville Road, now much altered. I lived at the far end of Wyngate Drive. During the war there was a large area of land here that had an air-raid shelter built on it. In the distance is John Hudson's horticultures.

Hinckley Road and Mostyn Street corner in 1956. The Co-op was just around the corner and Barclay's Bank was later built on this corner site. I remember a school friend, Jean Rollinson, whose father had an allotment on the Gimson Road site.

SECTION FOUR

People

Her Majesty the Queen in Victoria Park inspecting a guard of honour in May 1958 when she made a six-hour visit to the city accompanied by the Duke of Edinburgh. The demand to see the royal couple was so great that the city transport authorities needed to lay on 220 buses to take the crowds home afterwards.

A civil defence team holding the 'Warren Stanger' shield on location at the training field. I am fourth from left while second from left is Bob Rodd.

The marriage of Mr and Mrs Sid Wallace. Sid worked for G. Folwell as a pork pie maker and his wife Mary for Dunlop in the cycle tyre department. Other guests pictured, from left to right, are: Mrs Ena Faulkner, Ann Faulkner, Mr Frank England, Sid, Mary, Beryl Faulkner, Mr Wallace, and Mrs B. Wallace Snr. Mr Reg Faulkner, who took the photograph, was married to Ena Faulkner who worked for Oliver's Shoes for fifty years.

John Burton, Christopher Wompra and Alan Copson play in the back garden of 103 Wyngate Drive.

In this photograph taken in about 1912 and believed to be of West Bridge Wharf, men scoop out coal which has spilled into the canal over many years from passing trains.

Alderman Amos Sherriff, Leicester's first Lord Mayor in 1922, and Mrs Sherriff hand out free Christmas dinners at the Swain Street workhouse.

The Wyggeston hospital annual founders' day service in 1982. Left to right: Lord Lanesborough, the Very Reverend Alan Warren, the Lord Mayor Bill Page, Peter Clark, Harold Heard and Mrs Joan Page the Lady Mayoress. Harold Heard kept a butcher's shop on Hinckley Road.

VE day celebrations in May 1945. This photograph was taken in Camden Road at the Victory VE party. Among those pictured are the Vann family, Mr and Mrs Calow, Gwen Calow and Silvia Askins.

The back garden of a house in Bisley Street. The three ladies are, from left to right: Flori Dobson, Lilian Dobson and Edith Dobson. Flori's daughter, Mrs Mary Sharman, lives in the Abbey Lane area.

On tour in Cornwall in 1935. Mr and Mrs F. Wright, pictured on the far right, came from Stretton Road. Mr Wright worked at the County Court in Newarke Street.

A tree planting ceremony in Victoria Park, possibly to celebrate Queen Victoria's diamond jubilee in 1897. Councillor J. Herbert Marshall was Mayor at the time.

Third year students at Vaughan College in St Nicholas Way in 1984. They are, back row, left to right: Rekha Singh, Tony Sulley, Ruth Hadfield, Dan Clelland, David Geary, John Jones, Grace Youngs and Jane Taylor. Front row: Cheryl Norris, Kathryn Poachin, Anne Kemp, Lilian Boden, Rosemary Mans and Pauline Merrick.

Leicester's Lord Mayor Bernard Toft officially opens the Cheapside precinct. Leicester Rotary Club paid for the landscaping and the placement of the historic High Cross which was moved from the gardens of Newarke House Museum. Originally it had stood at the junction of the High Street and Highcross Street.

The staff of the Leicester lunatic asylum which was built at the top of Knighton Hill in 1837 and closed in 1907. The new asylum was built at Narborough. The Knighton Hill building was used as a military hospital during the First World War and was then bought by T. Fielding Johnson and presented to the university.

Chilprufe Quarter Century Club in East Park Road. The four new twenty-five-year members are Mrs Doris Cheeseman, Mrs Nora Russell, Mrs Eva Davies and Mr John Bollands. On the right is Mr G.W. Harris who made the presentations.

Dunlop St Mary's Mills retired employees' evening. Left to right: Edward Hammond, Mr and Mrs Bert Williamson, Mrs Florrie Madder and Mr Sydney Tite.

A clutch of clerics: the occasion for this photograph of 1942 is not known, but left to right in the front row are: Dr Garbett, Archbishop of York; Dr Temple, Archbishop of Canterbury; the Bishop of Leicester and the Lord and Lady Mayoress.

The wedding of Sidney and Margaret Haslum in 1934. They were married at the church of the Sacred Heart in Mere Road.

The workforce of Dingley's shoe tip factory in Ruby Street. The owner 'Tom' Dingley is still remembered by many as a very dear and kind master. He is in the picture as are Mrs Bella Cummings, Mrs Smart, Mr H. Ward, Mrs Ingram, Mrs Springthorpe, Mrs Alice Evans, Mrs Sharpe and Mr William Wheeler.

Thomas Cook, founder of the popular travel company. Edward Shipley Ellis and other directors of the Midland Railway were staunch supporters of the Leicester Temperance Society whose secretary, Thomas Cook, arranged trips for the members. The train fare to Loughborough in 1841 was 1s return. From these small beginnings the travel company of Thomas Cook & Son began to grow.

MR. EMERY.
Reporter.
· MR. Hy. NORMAN.
· MR. P. WARDLE.
· MR. CHALLIS.
· MR. BARFIELD, Sculptor.

6· MR. SCOTT,
Fire Brigade Chief
7· MR. ATKINS,
Reporter
8· MR. J.W. BURTO[n]
9· MR. KING VAN[n]
Foreman of Work

Taken by Oliver Burton.

MR. JOHN BURTON LAYING CORNER STONE OF CLOCK TOWER, MARCH 16th 1868.

John Burton lays the foundation stone of the Clock Tower on 16 March 1868. Others pictured are: Mr Emery, Mr Henry Norman, Mr P. Wardle, Mr Challis, Mr Barfield, Mr Scott, Mr Atkins, Mr J.W. Burton and Mr King Vann. Few people can imagine what the inside of the Clock Tower is like: less than 5 feet square, in a high vertical shaft, the sunlight filters through narrow slit windows. The original clock cost about £200 from Gillett & Bland of Croydon, and it is now in the Newarke House Museum. This photograph was taken by Oliver Burton.

Thomas Palmer and his wife Ruth with Dusty the dog, pictured in their garden at 18 Pool Road, off Fosse Road North, in the early 1900s.

Evans Lifts Quarter Century Club's annual dinner in 1972. In the front row, from left to right, are: Mr G. Page, Mr R.H. Blunt, Mr J. Page and Mr R. Barker. Back row: Mr A. Lewin, Mr W. Essex, Mr J. Sharman, Mr G. Williamson, Mr W. Brownett and Mr K. Naylor.

This is the sort of dust cart I first remember, with canvas fold-back tops; the later ones had metal slides. The rubbish was thrown in and pushed back with a wooden pusher. From left to right are: K.P. Williams, R. Childs, C.H. Smart and W. Bradwell, pictured in Victoria Park Road.

Members of the Anchor Tenants' Building Department in 1909. At the extreme left is G. Hearn, and on the extreme right is Sam Wilford. Others pictured are Fat Dan, Mr Taylor, R. Law, W. Pawley, A. Wilford and Mr Darby. Their motto – 'not greater wealth, but simpler pleasures'.

The kindergarten class at Belmont House School in about 1878. Some of those pictured are Miss Jones (in white blouse), Percy Gee on her knee, Ernest Walker, Somers Ellis and Poppy Gee. The school later became the Belmont Hotel.

Pictured at a party to celebrate their long service for R. Rowley & Co. Ltd are, from left to right: Mrs Flo Sewell, Mrs Gracie Gamble and Mrs Lucy Wilkinson, all holding bouquets. I worked with Flo and Lucy in C Department, which was a 'broadening education' to a fifteen-year-old just out of school; and I well remember the humour of Lucy and Bertha – two lovely ladies.

The Royal Oak in Colton Street, *c.* 1900, where Sarah Audley was the lady of the house. It was one of four public houses in this 200-yard-long street.

Brian Thompson (first left), chairman of the *Leicester Mercury*, with Nathan Harris of the Leicestershire Education Committee, presenting awards to students for the centenary project in 1975. On the right is Mr R. Tyldesley, managing director, and Mr N. Stack, editor. Also pictured are Christopher Bishop, Paul Kearns, Jefferson Cann, Diane Towers, Ramson Khan Awan, Autum Cooper, David Jewell and Alan Pugh.

SECTION FIVE

Transport

A Hansom cab in the 1930s beneath the Clock Tower. Joseph A. Hansom, its inventor, came originally from Hinckley and drove the cab to London to prove its worth.

Frears's baker's van in 1926. On the right, with his foot on the wheel, is George Coley aged about fourteen.

Price's bread delivery boy Tom Mould with his horse and cart. The bread is advertised as being 'self digestive'. Tom was killed in the battle of Passchendaele in 1916 aged twenty-six.

Don Rossa driving one of the many ice-cream vans which once plied the city streets. Ralph Rossa, founder of the company, bought redundant funeral hearses and converted them to ice-cream vans. Tony Rossa is seated in the back.

F.W. Coleman owned the Old North End Steam Bakery in Dunton Street. Mr White is holding the horse outside St Leonard's vicarage in Woodgate in 1914.

St Stephen's church – but where? The answer is next to the Midland station in London Road. In 1894 it was taken down stone by stone and rebuilt in De Montfort Street.

Wallace Arthur Cooke of 93 Belper Street at the helm of tramcar No. 118 to East Park Road. Mr Cooke was a tram driver for thirty-eight years before he retired in 1942, and was ninety-four years old when he died.

All change: wartime 'clippies' are shown how to change the points for their tramcars.

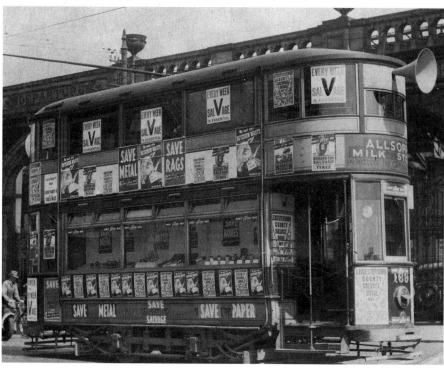

Tramcar No. 169 outside the Midland station on London Road in May 1942, decorated for the Leicestershire County Salvage Drive. This car was originally delivered unpainted in 1920 from the United Electric Car Co. of Preston.

Tramcar No. 76 has been restored and can be seen today at Crick. It took eight years of hard work to bring it to this magnificent state. When it was retired from service in 1949 it became a cricket pavilion and then a hen house, before its restoration.

Leicester Tramway Corporation employees outside the tram depot on Abbey Park Road in 1942.

An old and very rare postcard of the Midland station in the London Road.

This is the tower wagon of Leicester City Transport at work in Granby Street taking down forty miles of almost pure copper wire after the final withdrawal of trams from the city streets.

A BSA CII motorcycle in 1954, with Father Sheil in the saddle and ready for the off.

It is April 1958 and the Leicester Motor Scooter Club are off to tour Rutland from their Humberstone Gate meeting place.

This outing for the local cigar merchants in a De Dion Bouton was organized by P.L. Baker Tobacco Co. Pictured from left to right are: Edgar Reeve, Tom Allen, Alfred Catlow, Harry Webb, Percy Baker, Thomas Turner, William Robinson and William Sykes. In 1900 there were twenty-eight cigar firms in Leicester.

Charles Street traffic lights in about 1950. The vintage car in the foreground is called Priscilla, forty-four years old, with 'Old John' as the passenger.

The riders of ancient bicycles and tricycles in the Lord Mayor's show are Keith Gilbert, Graham Wills, David Packham, Clive Alexander and John Richards.

A 1901 Sunbeam Mabley, driven here by Ian Lynam, on its way from Victoria Park to Donnington Park.

A selection of old vehicles in the vicinity of the Thomas Cook building. They appear to be chauffeur-driven, but the occasion is not known.

Headley's baker's transport whose premises were in Andrews Street. The business was started in 1796 and taken over by Pitcher's in 1940. Headley's owned the pavilion café on Western Park and Anne, Thomas Headley's sister, ran it.

One of Leicester's early horse-drawn tramcars on its route to Narborough Road in about 1937.

SECTION SIX
Places of Interest

An etching of Westcotes, the seat of the Ruding family. A. Walter Ruding died in 1655 although the directory of 1815 lists an A. Walter Ruding of Westcotes.

The plaque on William Carey's cottage in Harvey Lane reads: 'This was William Carey's cottage, one of the greatest missionaries of all time. He said "expect great things from God, Attempt great things for God". And so he lived, and died, highly valued by so many.'

The Reverend Dr A.H. Kirby, President of Leicester Free Church Council, points out the plaque on William Carey's cottage to a party of Australian visitors.

More than sixty local people of various denominations were present in 1968 when the Reverend Hubert Janisch, a descendant of William Carey, blessed the building before its demolition.

A view inside Carey's cottage, taken in 1957.

The Parliament House in Red Cross Street. Local tradition identified it as the house to which the commons were directed to elect a speaker at the time parliament met in the castle.

On the corner of Marlborough Street and Welford Road stood the Welford Coffee House. This was a favourite place for newly discharged prisoners to get used to the outside world.

The old Wyggeston hospital seen from St Martin's churchyard. It was demolished in 1876.

Wyggeston hospital in about 1880, in the grounds bordered by Fosse Road and Hinckley Road.

The site for the new X-ray and casualty department of the Leicester Royal Infirmary in the 1950s.

The entrance hall to the Royal Infirmary, viewed in the 1920s.

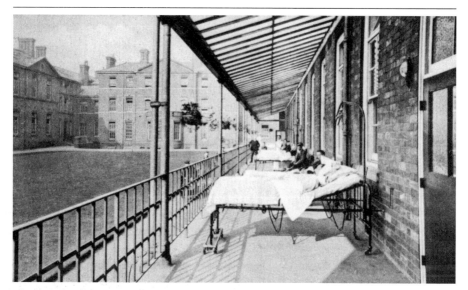

The Royal Infirmary's open air balcony, *c.* 1920.

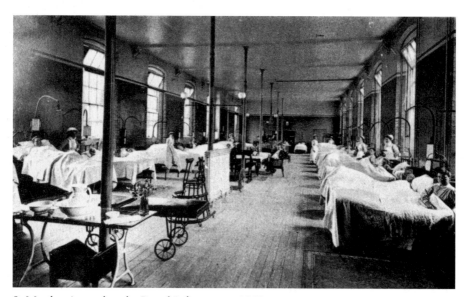

St Matthew's ward at the Royal Infirmary, *c.* 1920.

Leicester Royal Infirmary nurses' chapel was opened in 1888 to provide a quiet corner for prayer and contemplation.

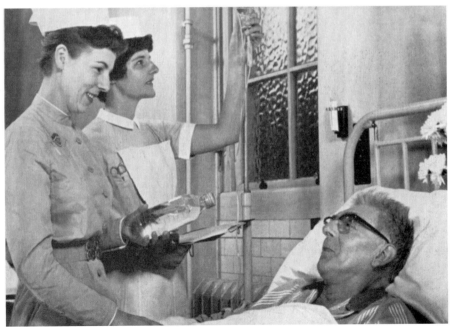

A friendly word from Sister in 1966.

The Hillcrest hospital for the elderly pictured in December 1965.

This is the minimum care ward at the Hillcrest hospital. Unfortunately the names of these grand old ladies are unknown.

The Towers hospital was a magnificent building, but holds bad memories for me and many others.

Thomas Collinson with his wife Sarah and family pose for the photographer in front of The Old Red Lion at Sanvey Gate. His son Frank is on the right.

The grounds of the Leicester Municipal building, seen here in about 1918, was a place for the city centre workers to sit and reflect at lunchtime on a sunny day.

The old free school in Highcross Street, seen here in 1954 after its change of use to a warehouse.

Vaughan College in Vaughan Way gave 100 years of service to the city. One of my teachers, Eric Swift, lectured at the evening classes held here.

The weighbridge in the Haymarket is better known as Humberstone Gate. The last machine, with a capacity of 20 tons, was installed in 1927.

Freeman Hardy & Willis in Rutland Street was bombed in the Second World War, but the coffee stall survived.

The Duke of Rutland lays the foundation stone for a new wing of the Royal Infirmary in 1907. The first building was opened in 1771.

The Midland station, *c.* 1906. Evidently it was a busy time for horse-drawn vehicles.

Winn's café in the Market Place where I was sometimes taken to tea by my father Arthur Burton, who worked at R. Morley & Sons. The café had a musical trio who played 'softly, very posh' to the patrons.

Lyndhurst College was in Highfields on the corner of Gotham Street and Highfield Street, where Miss Edith Elizabeth Saunders LRAM and Miss Nora Cranfield were the principals from 1922. The school moved to Knighton Park Road in 1941.

These two stone orphans have stood together since 1790 in their alcove above the main entrance to St Martin's Church of England School in Friar Lane. The school closed shortly after the picture was taken in 1957.

Robert Stephenson, son of the famous railway pioneer, designed this lifting bridge. It is dated 1834 and the central section lifted to allow barges to go underneath.

SECTION SEVEN
Leisure and Sport

The Abbey ruins in Abbey Park, pictured in about 1942. Cardinal Wolsey died here some four hundred years earlier.

This peaceful scene is at Western Park near the bowling green, where a horse-drawn grass cutter driven by F. Rodwell is pulled by Betty in the sunshine of 1959.

Spinney Hill Park is the tranquil setting for a quiet stroll by the water in 1940.

The canals played a vital role in the history of Leicester as they were once the motorways of industry. This view of Frog Island in 1908 shows barges in the Northgate Locks, and ladies in traditional dress.

The Pavilion Theatre in the centre of Leicester once played a principal part in the city's theatrical history, although the building has long since gone. Note the shop on the right that sells corn, flour and pig food.

Kenwood swimming pool, seen here in its heyday, has since been demolished and the site transformed into a housing estate.

In November 1968 former Leicester City players put on their kit for a game against Newfoundpool WMC at Birstall, to raise money for club funds. From left to right in the back row are: Jimmy McLaughlan, Jimmy Walsh, Johnny Anderson, Ken Chisolm, Derek Hogg, Walter Harrison, Jimmy Harrison and Norman Plummer. The front row are: Adam Dickson, Charles Adam, Ted Jelly and Ron Jackson.

The Sunday school football team, otherwise known as the 'wicked west-enders'. In the back row, from left to right, are: the Reverend W.E. Hurst of Robert Hall Memorial Chapel, Bert Cross, Albert Northfold, Matt Flude, T. Hadwell. Middle row: Joe Hincks (Josia Hincks, solicitors), Alfred Deighton, Stan Jackson, Alec Chilton. Front row: Alfred Hambleton, J. Martin, Arthur Houghton, Harry Warrington, J. Marshall.

Westcotes Congregational church cricket club in 1929. Left to right, from the back: A.E. Lines, W.T. Garrett, A. Hill, S.V. Smith, E. Tyler, W.A. Baines, R. Faulkner, J.E. Green, R.S. Taylor, G.D. Langham, R.H. Blakesley, J. Linnett. Reg Faulkner (see p. 99) was my father-in-law.

Leicester Tigers. Standing from left to right are: P.C.S. Pulfrey, J. Quick, K.P. Andrews, P.W.G. Tom, R. Beason, M. Bedgood, F.L.J. Walton and W.M. Bussey. Seated from left to right are: M.J. Harrison, J.A. Allen, K. Chilton, D.J. Matthews (Capt), M.R. Walker, R.W. Small and D.W. Bird. This was the team that beat Oxford University 14/11 in October 1965.

Pre-war grass track racing in 1929. Fourth from the left, riding a 350cc Velocette at a track near Lutterworth, is Leslie Wilford who was employed by the *Leicester Mercury* as a despatch rider. Sadly it is not possible to identify the other riders.

The Leicester Hunters speedway team won the first Midland Cup in 1951 when they defeated Birmingham. Their home at Blackbird Road stadium closed in 1984 after fifty-six years of sporting activity.

One of the saddest scenes for many was the demolition of the Theatre Royal. I can still remember Ray Mort and Billie Whitelaw in rep shows there.

Acknowledgements

My thanks go to the many people who have helped in the preparation of this book. First of all to my wife Beryl for her encouragement and help; to Annie and Stuart Burton for typing and computer services; to Ann and Michael Potter of Oadby, to Albert and Mary Sharman of Abbey Lane, to Mark and Tony Witcher, and to Mr R.A. Jelley; to the management and staff of the *Leicester Mercury*, and to Steve England and his colleagues in the library department. To all of you a very sincere thank-you.

David R. Burton